CELL 170

Ministering in Prison

CELL 170
DEANNA HAMES

TATE PUBLISHING
AND ENTERPRISES, LLC

Published by Tate Publishing & Enterprises, LLC
127 E. Trade Center Terrace | Mustang, Oklahoma 73064 USA
1.888.361.9473 | www.tatepublishing.com

Tate Publishing is committed to excellence in the publishing industry. The company reflects the philosophy established by the founders, based on Psalm 68:11,
"The Lord gave the word and great was the company of those who published it."

Book design copyright © 2013 by Tate Publishing, LLC. All rights reserved.
Cover design by Jan Sunday Quilaquil
Interior design by Ronnel Luspoc

Published in the United States of America

ISBN: 978-1-62510-676-6
1. Biography & Autobiography / General
2. Religion / Christian Ministry / General
12.12.10

To all those who are incarcerated.

Acknowledgements

I will be forever grateful to Stacy Baker at Tate Publishing for believing in me and giving me the chance to share my experiences of God's Saving Grace. Many thanks as well to Mr. Richard Tate, CEO of Tate Publishing, who took the time to sit down with me on my first visit and share stories that let me see what a good Christian man he was and help me feel comfortable. To my family and friends for having faith in me to bring into written words the love God has for all His children. To my husband Jim, without whose love I could never have accomplished such an undertaking. I will always be thankful for the help and joy my granddaughters Danielle, Ashley, and Cayla have brought to me throughout the writing of this book. I am uplifted by the love and compassion demonstrated by them as they helped me prepare meals to take to the prison and wrote notes of encouragement to the prisoners, as well as helping me with anything I asked of them, as did their mother Lisa. I am so blessed. I appreciate those who read pieces of the book and encouraged me to keep going: Steve and Helen Hames; Adam and Lisa Hames; Patti Grubb; Kelli McFadden; Mindi Okewole; Beth Hathaway; Ann Clifton; Debbie and Butch Finnell;

Eric Hames; Jan Hunter; Kathy Cox; Billie and Leesa Hames; Deacon Kenny Longbrake; Deacon Jeff and Mary Lynn Willard; Patti Vincent; Clare Maehs.

Table of Contents

Preface

Having been writing this book over a span of 5 years has been rewarding as well as challenging at times. I have had memories enter my mind, some I would have forgotten had I not started a book. Often times these memories come at inopportune times such as in the grocery store, at a movie theater, or while cooking dinner. These were times I had no easy access to record them at that very moment, and feared they would exit my mind as quickly as they had entered. But with the help and encouragement of my dear husband, who I give credit to for leading me into this amazing ministry of compassionate love, I have been able to continue writing.

I have changed the names of those I have written about, and apologize to ones I have left out. All the events in here really happened. For those who are familiar with these stories, please forgive persons or details I failed to mention.

As human beings, we have a connection to one another, because of our being made in the image and likeness of God. I have seen that image in my husband, my children, my grand children, extended family, and friends. And I have now seen it in the faces of my incarcerated brothers that I have come to know & love. But before you can see that image in others, you must first see it in yourself. People who are in prison, are just *people*…in prison.

CHAPTER I

First Prison Visit

My first time to see the inside of a prison was in 1978. The principal of the small country school my two sons had attended, since kindergarten and third grade, thought it a good idea to take the eighth grade students, one was my oldest son Steve, inside the Oklahoma State Prison in McAlester, for part of their eighth grade trip. Having watched a popular television documentary called Scared Straight, he asked for parents to go along as chaperones and there were around five of us that volunteered, and had seen the documentary as well. The subject of the documentary was the introduction of a group of teenage delinquents to actual convicts, with the objective being to make the teens end their criminal ways. Our objective also was a possible deterrent to crime and to keep our kids on the path to becoming productive citizens. Our trip was to be educational, as well as fun by first spending the night at Robbers Cave in southeastern Oklahoma near McAlester. Robber's Cave was an appropriate beginning and place to start our trip. It is located in the picturesque San Bois Mountains and became a park in 1935. The "claim to fame" for Robber's Cave is as a legendary hideout for infamous Old West outlaws. Some names associated with the cave in local legend are Jesse James and Belle Starr.

It was a beautiful, sunny day as we arrived by school bus, at the Robber's Cave campgrounds, where we would be spending the night. As we unloaded, everyone was anxious to get settled in so we could start our planned activities of fishing, hiking, and exploring the cave and natural wonder of the park. We had a picnic lunch outside under a clear blue sky. The day was perfect; no wind, and a stillness you could almost reach out and touch.

The only noise was the sound of happy, carefree children talking, laughing, and squealing as they dipped their bare feet in the cool water from the stream that ran behind our cabins. The day was filled with fun and freedom, roly-poly bugs, butterflies, getting dirty, and it being okay. There was a feeling of being one with nature, feeling liberated, some of the kids said. School was over, for the summer at least, and they realized this was a chapter in their lives they would not experience again. Some would go their separate ways to different high schools, and perhaps some might move away and this would be the last time they would all be together and they made the best of it. The day proved to be as carefree as it was beautiful and sunny and it was a celebration of their years together as students and friends.

After a fun-filled day, we began to prepare our evening meal and our thoughts had already settled on the stories that would be told around the campfire later that night. Most of them were scary stories we parents had heard as children from our parents and were now passing them on to our kids. A campfire, clothes hangers with roasted marshmallows dangling off the ends, ghost stories being told as if they were true, kids getting sleepy from a fun filled day, exhausted grownups wrapping things up and getting children settled in for the night. It had been a very good day. Hopefully, tomorrow would be just as successful as we headed toward our destination, the Oklahoma State Penitentiary. With our goodnights having been said, even a cabin bunk and a sleeping bag looked good to all of us.

After a night of exhausted, but somewhat restful sleep, morning came a little too soon for us parents. But after getting a simple breakfast of muffins and juice underway and with everyone helping clean up, it wasn't long before it was time to gather principal, parents, children, belongings and bus driver together, board the bus and head for the prison, often referred to as "The Walls." Unlike the sun filled day before, the cloudy sky was dark and dreary, but even with the threat of rain hanging overhead, it didn't seem to dampen anyone's enthusiasm. Yesterday was gone but not it's memories. Good memories last a lifetime. The kids seemed to be almost overly excited and this concerned us a little. So, we tried to instill in the students a healthy fear, if there is one, and the serious nature of this part of our trip. But, being 13-year-olds and still wound up from late night ghost stories and sugary toasted marshmallows, they seemed very disinterested in our instructions as to their conduct, while inside the prison. But the realization of the facility we were about to enter soon appeared to them and all of us as our bus driver pulled in to the prison parking lot and our eyes were met by the stark white and desolate looking building in front of us. It had walls surrounding it that looked ancient, yet strong. Everything was painted white, but was in dire need of a couple of fresh coats. The massive walls were surrounded by double rows of chain link fence, topped with double layers of razor wire and in every corner was a guard tower. To describe what I saw from the bus windows, for the very first time, it would be the word ominous. The definition of the word is "threatening; foreboding, as a bank of ominous looking clouds." *Much like those that had gathered overhead*, I thought to myself. Within those walls were 1,500 men, some of whom had committed the most heinous and despicable crimes imaginable. Ominous was a very descriptive word.

Since 1973, the prison yard had been closed due to one of the worse prison riots in history. Many factors led to the riot, with overcrowding heading the list as well as ill qualified and too few correctional officers and last but certainly not least, violence perpetrated by "convict bosses."

The prison was built in 1911 and was to have 1,100 inmates, but by 1920, the population was well over that number and it exceeded 2,200 by 1973. In July of 1973, the riot broke out and much violence erupted. A lieutenant and a captain were stabbed in the mess hall and were later treated at a hospital. The Deputy Warden and a prison official were the first hostages taken. The first inmate deaths occurred at 4:30 p.m. when two were stabbed and beaten by fellow inmates. The inmates took over the prison hospital at 5:35 p.m. and the prison was set on fire 25 minutes later. It was August 4th before the hostages were released and the prison was out of the inmates' control. In 1976, it reopened but by 1985, was shut down again, due to another riot. At that time, a 23-hour lock down was put into place and remains to this day, May 30, 2007. Only a handful of prisons nationwide lock their inmates in their cells 23 hours a day.

Only ten men at any one time are allowed out of their cells. During that one hour a day, they are permitted to take a shower or they are taken for some fresh air, to a very small area covered on all sides and topped by razor wire. From the moment we arrived, we were very aware of where we were and what we were about as parents and teachers. Yet, it would be years later before I would learn of this particular page in history of the prison we were about to enter.

To say that this was the beginning of a journey for me would be an understatement. We were processed at the front office, which took an extremely long time, before then going through metal detectors and finally being met by a staff member who briefed us before our eye opening tour began. We were split into two groups and my son happened to be with the other group. Although I felt anxious about this, I tried not to let it worry me too much. After all, we were now privy to the strict security measures taken with us and so felt pretty safe. The correctional officer leading my group, showed us various cell blocks and told us some of the history of the prison. It was built around the turn of the century, and not only did it look cold, stark and antiquated but you could almost feel and smell the evil that had been perpetrated in this place for close to three quarters of a century. I remember thinking to myself, "If these walls could talk, what stories they would tell."

We got a glimpse down the corridor where the inmates awaiting execution were housed, and a glimpse was plenty for me. Then the correctional officer asked if we wanted to see the room referred to as, "the dungeon." This was the room, where the executions had been carried out by electric chair, until 1970, when it was deemed too cruel and inhumane. *Was there really a kind and humane way to execute a person?* I thought to myself.

As we were led down the flight of stairs to the "dungeon," the colder and darker everything felt and looked to me. There was also an odor that was hard to describe. If the words cold, dark and metal have an odor, that's what it smelled like to me. Entering the room I froze; I almost lost my breath as I stood only a couple of feet away from the electric chair. It was a hideous looking device upon which so many had been brought to what is commonly believed to be justice. The chair was made of metal and tarnished from time and use. Hanging loosely off the arms were wide and very worn brown leather straps. They were worn from much use and the struggle to hold on to life as the electric current ran through the bodies of those condemned to die. Then as I looked down at the floor in front of the seat, I saw that the paint was worn off where feet had pushed at the floor. Ultimately death would win and to the world, justice would be served. But I knew that that was not how God wanted to mete out justice. As Scripture tells us, "Vengeance is Mine," says the Lord. After hearing a first hand account of witnessing an execution, by the correctional officer, we were all more than eager to leave the old and dank room and forget what we had just seen, felt, and heard. Little did I know then, that particular memory would never leave me.

While on our tour, something occurred that left me wondering if taking the children inside the prison had been a good decision. It happened during "count," that is various times during the day and night when the inmates have to account for their presence. One inmate, we were informed, was not accounted for and that meant that everything came to a standstill. The entire prison was put on "lockdown" until he was found. We were detained for over an hour and a half while the entire facility and vehicles in the parking lot were searched, including our school bus. Next, we were told the dogs would be turned out on the yard and I can still hear the barking and yelping as they scoured the prison for the missing man. At first, we all thought it was just part of the tour, used as a scare tactic for the benefit of the students. But that thought was short lived because we soon realized it was real. With my son and I in different areas of the prison at the time of the "lock down," needless to say, I was a little more than uncomfortable with the situation. I had to really talk to myself to calm my fears and not give in to the waves of panic that flooded over me during that hour and a half. We had absolutely no control over the predicament we found ourselves in and to make things worse, time seemed to drag on, much like it must for the inmates who call "The Walls" their home. But with time and a thorough search by the prison officials, the inmate was accounted for, and we were finally free to go. I was thankfully reunited with my son, once we were back on the bus. We all had much to talk about, and yet it was as though words escaped us as we left "The Walls" behind us. I may never know what kind of impact that visit made on the other students and parents, but I do know it affected my son and myself in a positive way, as time would tell. That would be the last tour that would be allowed at Oklahoma State Prison in McAlester, due to the Department of Corrections deeming it too dangerous and a matter of security.

CHAPTER II

Christmas Party

It would be twelve years before I would again go behind prison walls. My husband and I were asked by our good friends Melinda and Jesse to accompany them on a trip to the Oklahoma State Reformatory at Granite, Oklahoma to visit a family member of Melinda's who was incarcerated there. It was the Christmas season and the inmates and their families were allowed to find sponsors who would help them, by donating gifts to their families. We were more than happy to help out our friends and agreed to go as sponsors. The event was celebrated at the prison, with a Christmas party, which included the inmate's families, friends, and sponsors. I can remember everything clearly, as if it were only yesterday. The appearance of the prison was a lot like "The Walls" at McAlester, old, strong, with everything painted white years ago, so it too was in need of a new coat or two of fresh paint. It was built after the turn of the century by prison inmate labor and from the granite quarried from the mountain adjacent to it. Kate Bernard was Oklahoma Commissioner of Charities and Corrections in 1907, and within two years had persuaded the State Legislature to develop and build both Oklahoma State Prison at McAlester and Oklahoma State Reformatory at Granite. Although from the outside it was stark and foreboding, when you got inside the yard there were flower beds that in the springtime would be full of periwinkles and begonias as well as impatiens and geraniums, all planted and tended to by the inmates. I recall as the dinner and party got underway, there was a very festive mood. The food served by the prison kitchen staff was surprisingly good. The music was provided by a group of musicians who were inmates and they called themselves, "The Rock," which is also what the prison is nicknamed. The members of the band were quite talented, and as they played, while others ate and visited, the dance floor began to fill with the inmates and their wives or girlfriends and children. Before we began to eat our meal, my husband Jim was asked to say the blessing, and I remember as he prayed, I was amazed at the beautiful tone of his voice and how words of peace and love just seemed to flow freely from his mouth. Something Divine was happening at that moment, without our realizing exactly what it was. He was being prepared for the future role he would have in God's plan for us.

This day was a first, but by no means a last, experience for Jim and I. We spent time one on one with those who, for a multitude of reasons, had lost their way and turned to a life of drug abuse, violent, as well as non-violent crimes and oftentimes a near death experience of their souls. I thought it a little curious at the time, but I never felt terribly afraid or uncomfortable in that environment as I had at The Walls in McAlester. But I didn't have the responsibility of having my son as well as other children in my care this time. So I really gave that fact little thought because as far as I knew, I would never be inside a prison again. The day was a success for all involved and for a few hours, families were reunited and happy, if only for that brief time.

CHAPTER III

Beto Unit

In May of 1989 my youngest son Adam had married and given our family a lovely new member named Lisa, to love and cherish. From the tender age of twelve, I grew up in a male household, with my father and a brother 10 years older than I. My mother passed away due to heart disease at age fifty. At 16-years-old I married my husband Jim, the most handsome man, who turned out to be so much more. I've never known anyone more faithful, trustworthy, or dependable. I was then blessed with our two handsome sons, who have their father's wonderful attributes as well as some of their own. As I thought about this male world I lived in, a world of boys wrestling on the living room floor, football games, basketball practice, Cub Scouts, sleep outs in tents and tree houses, midnight trips to the marina to fish, I knew another female in the family would be different, but it would be a good thing. And so, Lisa was welcomed into our family with open arms. Both our sons had moved out at age 20, Steve first and then three years later Adam. With the "empty nest" syndrome in full swing at that time, I had gotten involved with a lot of volunteer work at our church. I was fortunate in the fact that I never had to work outside the home. Jim was a more than adequate provider for our family, and I am forever grateful for him. I joined the Women's Club, St Veronica's Guild, co-chaired the Thanksgiving Dinner at our parish, was a member of the Ministry of Care group by visiting those of our Parish who were hospitalized, and cooked meals for our priest. I was also very involved with a movement within the Catholic Church called Cursillo (a Spanish word meaning, "short course in Christianity.")

Four years later, June 30,1993, I became a grandmother for the first time. My son Adam and daughter-in-law Lisa had their first child, Danielle, a beautiful baby girl, with brown eyes that tell of the Choctaw Indian heritage of my mother, as does her pretty, shiny, and sleek brown hair and prominent cheekbones. As she has grown older she has proven to be just as beautiful inside as she is out. Danielle is not only intelligent, but has a great degree of "good old common sense", which is ranked highly in my family. She is very compassionate and kind. She is quite independent and headstrong as well, but in an amazing and gentle kind of way. When she makes up her mind, you can bet, it's made up. I tell her she's my favorite first granddaughter and that always makes her laugh. She has a great sense of humor and laughs easily. With her birth, I could feel the "nest" filling up again as the pull toward home and family became stronger than the need to be involved in so much volunteer work. That same year, a priest we had become acquainted with through Cursillo, asked my husband Jim to be the Catholic representative on an AD hoc committee, with the goal being to bring a program called Kairos into the Oklahoma Prison System. Kairos is a Greek word meaning "God's' Special Time." Jim accepted and through the meetings was connected with Ron and his wife Jane, and we became close friends. Ron and Jane had been trying for several years to bring Kairos to Oklahoma. The attempts had been unsuccessful due to the Ecumenical nature of the program requiring the signing of an agreement by Church leaders, some of whom would not support the program. Many years and many prayers later, the agreement was finally signed, and plans could move forward in "God's special time." After the third or fourth ad hoc committee meeting, Jim told me that he was going to Texas to observe a Kairos weekend and to see if prison ministry was something he wanted to be involved with. He asked me if I would be interested in going along. I thought about it and decided I would go and support Jim, but I had no intention of getting involved; after all, we were just going to observe. But, before I knew it, we were headed to Palestine, Texas, and a prison called Beto Unit #10. I was just along for the ride, or so I thought.

The Kairos program was born out of the Cursillo movement and was adapted to better meet the needs of the incarcerated. It is a program beginning on Thursday evening, which consists of meeting the 42 inmates. Kairos asks for 85% of the 42 to be negative leaders and 15% positive leaders, those who are attending church services and trying to live as Christians. The purpose being, if the 85% have an experience of God touching their lives, they can influence the other inmates in the prison and lives can be changed and souls saved. The 42 men have been chosen by the chaplain and unit managers to attend the weekend, which continues on Friday and Saturday with lay speakers and clergy witnessing to the power of God at work in their lives. There are also meditations, music, food, and lots of homemade cookies. The entire weekend is based on prayer, and is possible only through and because of God's unconditional love for all His children. On Sunday afternoon, the outside team, who have been cooking and praying, get to go inside the prison and attend the closing. This is an opportunity for the inmates to speak about the weekend and what they have experienced. Afterwards there is a short time for visiting with the inmates before they have to return to their cells and we have to leave the prison. After attending the closing and hearing the testimonies, we left Palestine, Texas, and those behind the walls of Beto Unit #10. Jim received the conviction in his heart that he indeed was called to this ministry and, to my surprise, I too was hooked and knew I was to have an active role in Kairos as well. We returned to Oklahoma with a mission and the message that God's love must reach those whom society would rather forget.

And so the wheels were set in motion as we helped form a team and prepared to bring God's unconditional love to 42 inmates behind the walls at the Oklahoma State Prison. Bringing Kairos into Oklahoma State Prison would prove to be a difficult task, but an attainable one because God willed it, and so the journey began.

CHAPTER IV

Weekend at the Walls

Preparation for a Kairos weekend at Oklahoma State Prison started by having a series of eight team meetings, one every week end for eight weeks. During these meetings, the goal was to form authentic Christian community among the various Protestant and Catholic team members. This was accomplished by sharing, praying, working together, making plans, and working out the many details for the weekend to be a success. We worked as if everything depended on us, and prayed as though everything depended on God. There were speakers for the various talks, clergy persons, music minister, prayer teams, an inside and outside coordinator, kitchen manager, and even a cookie chairperson that had to be chosen. It seemed an enormous challenge at times. It was decided that our friend Ron would assume the position of Rector while Jim would be coordinator. Ron's wife Jane and I worked on the outside team doing many jobs including sacking, into bags of one dozen each, five thousand dozen cookies for the weekend, to be distributed to all 1500 inmates.

I was the cookie chairperson and I had learned at Beto that you had to have a strategy and a method for getting that many cookies sacked and distributed. Unbeknownst to me, there were a couple of other ladies on the team who had their own method and strategy and each one was different and no one seemed willing to listen to me. This caused a lot of confusion and a lot of time spent re-doing, re-sacking, and re-boxing the cookies. The prison had in place, a strict criteria we had to adhere to, and it included the way the cookies were sent into the prison. Since we were getting nowhere fast, the kitchen manager and I had a meeting and we informed the team sacking the cookies that they would have to follow my instructions or we would not get enough cookies sacked for all the men to receive them on both Friday and Saturday. We let the ladies know that even if they were sure they had a better way than mine, now was not the time to try out their methods. By Friday evening it became evidently clear to me, we could not get enough cookies sacked. So, Saturday morning before Jim left for the prison, I asked him to inform Deputy Warden Uland, with whom we had been working closely, that we wouldn't be sending cookies in today.

Around mid-morning the kitchen manager told me I had a call from the prison. It was Warden Uland, and he wanted to know the reason the cookies would not be sent in. I told him we simply didn't have enough people or time to get the job done. "Deanna," he said, " We have had riots over less issues than this. We must have the cookies. The men have been promised cookies and cookies they will have." He then asked me how many people I thought we needed to finish the job. I told him maybe we could get it done with another five or six people, but we didn't have five or six people. He told me not to worry, which I thought was an odd statement in light of our conversation, but within thirty minutes, six of his office staff were walking through the door, asking what we needed to do to get the cookies into the prison and into the hands and mouths of the men who anxiously awaited them. Needless to say, I was thankful and relieved. I certainly did not want to make the McAlester newspaper headlines reading something like, "Norman woman in charge of cookie ministry to "The Walls" fails to deliver the goods causing riot to break out among inmates." Although I can joke about this incident now, it was no joke when Warden Uland called me that morning.

On Saturday night, as the inmates go back to their cells, they are given a sack of cookies and asked to give them to the person they need to forgive the most. The men have said they give them to someone who has been harassing them, to a particularly hard to get along with correctional officer, the warden, any one they have not yet forgiven. One young man said he kept the cookies for himself, because he had never forgiven himself for what he had done. We have heard countless stories of healing and forgiveness,

God's grace and mercy being poured out, through a sack full of cookies of all things. The chaplain later told us, he had never seen it so quiet and peaceful, even months after the Kairos weekend. Years later, we would hear from a man who was a case manager there, at the same time we had the Kairos weekend. He told my husband Jim that they averaged two stabbings a week at the prison, but that for months after Kairos left there was not a single one.

Sunday morning, the team arose tired yet anxious as to what the day would bring. There would be obstacles to overcome as there had been all weekend, but out of it all would come blessings, graces, and miracles as we looked forward to seeing and hearing the men, who had come in on Thursday evening with hearts of stone, witness to the transforming power of God's unconditional love, at the closing. It was all we had hoped and prayed for and more and we gave God the praise and glory. Lives were changed that weekend. We acknowledged that with God all things are possible.

There were so many happenings that occurred out of the ordinary against prison regulations and rules that weekend, that made us know what we were doing was definitely of God. This prison is one of the toughest and yet those in charge of this facility were allowing rules to be broken to accommodate us. At one time the warden, deputy warden, and the head of security were all in the same area where the team and inmates were. This was not their normal procedure, as they never put all those in charge of security in the same place at the same time. They obviously felt secure in doing this and when God is in charge extraordinary things occur. My husband Jim asked for something to cut the bananas with for banana splits they were serving them and the head of security sent one of the correctional officers to the kitchen and he brought back a butcher knife. Jim said his eyes almost popped out of his head when he saw it. But he certainly got the bananas cut in half. Ask and he did receive.

In April 1995, we had our van partially packed and ready to leave for what was to be the second Kairos weekend at Oklahoma State Prison at McAlester. The phone rang and the call was from the prison Chaplain. He informed us that the weekend had been postponed due to the bombing of the Murrah Federal Building in Oklahoma City. They were sending all of their extra people there to help out with the grave situation and there would not be enough security at the prison to ensure our safety. As we unpacked our van, the disappointment of the weekend being cancelled was overshadowed by the sorrow of what had happened at the Murrah Building. Lives had been lost; lives had been changed forever, because of one senseless act of violence. A friend and fellow Kairos volunteer, Chris Miracle, who was a counselor, was lending his services to those devastated by what had happened, especially those closest to the victims. As members of humankind, I think we all felt devastated and victimized. We received a call from Chris, and he asked if we could accommodate him by letting him stay with us during this time. We counted it as a privilege and the least we could do. That year a new warden was hired at the prison and he was not supportive of Kairos so unfortunately that was the last time we were to have a Kairos weekend at Oklahoma State Prison.

We had our second Kairos in the fall of 1995, at Oklahoma Reformatory at Granite Oklahoma, another first for us. Again, Jim was the coordinator and I did various jobs along with Jane. I had given everyone on the outside team the name of an inside team member to be praying for, as well as the 42 inmates and prison staff. My friend Jane and I promised to pray for one another's husband; she would pray for Jim and I would be praying for Ron. The work was sometimes very tiring for the outside team as well as those on the inside. We were doing all our cooking at a local church kitchen. We cooked and delivered to the prison, two meals a day for the 42 inmates attending the weekend, the prison staff, and the Kairos team members, totaling over 120 people. We also cooked breakfast for the team and had sandwiches and snacks ready for them as they returned to the church around 9 o'clock in the evening. Most of the team members stayed at the church during the weekend, sleeping on the floor and sometimes getting only four or five hours of sleep a night.

Taking a much-needed break on Friday afternoon, I slipped over to the church and laid down on one of the pews. It was cool, dark, and quiet as I began to pray asking God to be with Jim and our friend Ron. All of a sudden, with my eyes shut, I began to see a series of numbers before me. Startled, I sat up, opened my eyes and they were gone from my sight but not my memory. I wasn't sure what it meant and then it occurred to me that what I had seen must be one of the inmate's number. I prayed, "Lord, I don't know who these numbers belong to, but you do, so please be with them and let them feel your presence." After I had rested a few more minutes, I went back to work and later that day mentioned to Jane my experience over in the church. She asked me if I remembered any of the numbers I had seen. I said I remembered all of them and told her what they were. She just stood there, looking shocked. "Jane," I said, "what is it?" "Those were Ron's numbers when he served time in the Federal Prison in El Reno," she said. "But how did you know?" was her question. " I didn't," was my reply, "God did and He knew Ron needed my prayers at that moment."

We had many more powerful moments during OSR #1, but the most grace-filled for me was the closing. From the time we left the church and headed out to the prison, I was filled with excitement and anticipation of seeing and hearing the miracles through God's unconditional love that had been poured out upon those who had thought all hope was lost. Earlier I mentioned going to Oklahoma State

Reformatory with our friends for the Christmas party and that they had a family member who was incarcerated there. God in His Goodness allowed this young man to attend the Kairos weekend here at OSR. With God all things are possible. The Kairos team had been the hands and feet of Christ that weekend, and would be for many more to come. God's saving love through Kairos would soon spread throughout the Oklahoma Prison System. Needless to say, I was hooked alright, but not without struggles yet to come. You see, I still wanted and believed that I needed to devote all my time to my family. My oldest son had just gotten married to a beautiful woman named Helen and added another gift to our family to love and cherish. And to our family yet another gift was added, Margaret Ann, Helen's daughter, another member to love and cherish. God is good.

Apparently, I was not in charge of how involved with this prison ministry I would become. Try as I might to find excuses, every time Jim worked a team, I was there as well. While I was profoundly moved by the effect the power of God's love had on these men, by the time I was home again after each weekend, I would tell myself that I just couldn't work the next time. Once again, I was all about family, and I even felt a little guilty about being gone. What if a family member needed me, and I wasn't there for them? This fear came, I believe, from losing my mother at such an early age. With our precious granddaughter Danielle now 2-years-old, and our precious second granddaughter, Ashley, a darling curly blond haired and deep blue eyed child, on the way, I believed strongly in the old African adage that says, "it takes a whole village to raise a child." Having lost my mother at the young age of 12, I felt as the grandmother, I had a very important role in our village. With Ashley's birth I felt the blessing once again of joy. With curly blond hair and blue eyes, she takes her coloring after Lisa's side of the family, who are Polish and Hungarian, yet she and Danielle favor in many ways. Ashley is intelligent as well as beautiful inside and out. She has a good sense of humor and laughs easily, like her sister, especially when I tell her she's my favorite second granddaughter. She has her opinion and doesn't mind voicing it and has good common sense. She is a very kind and gentle soul. Only time would tell how my role would intensify and I would be needed more. Our daughter-in-law Lisa's mother, Veronica, had been diagnosed with cancer in 1991. She was with the grandchildren as much as she could be, while still working a 9 to 5 job as well. She was a very strong woman and would live to see our precious third granddaughter, Cayla, who has pretty light brown hair and beautiful blue eyes, enter this world and reach her eight month birthday, before Veronica would receive God's ultimate healing and be taken to her Heavenly home. Cayla reminds me of her grandmother Veronica in her looks and is a little more serious in nature like her mother. She is athletic and loves sports and is quite good. She has a mind of her own, yet can be as loving and dear as her sisters She laughs as well as her sisters when I tell her she's my favorite third granddaughter. I try to do my part in keeping their grandmother's memory alive by recalling little things I remember about her and telling them what a wonderful person she was and how much she loved them and still does. I miss her very much.

CHAPTER V

Answered Prayer

The next Kairos at OSR proved to be just as miraculous and powerful as the previous one. We all got just as tired as before, but now we knew and looked forward, with a Holy excitement and anticipation, to Sunday afternoon's closing. Our oldest son Steve and wife Helen worked with us on this weekend, so we had an added blessing to be thankful for this time. Steve worked on the team as a music minister, playing guitar, with our friend Vince. Helen was with me on the kitchen team.

At the closing an inmate named Tim, who said it was the best weekend he had spent in his entire life, shared that he had only signed up to attend the weekend because he heard there would be good food and "women." We all got quite a laugh out of that because except for my daughter-in-law, the average age of us "women" was 50-years-old. But Tim went on to say that he had found something he had not expected. He found God's Love and a community of people who showed him that love. I had started a list of those inmates God had put on my heart to say special prayers for at OSP #1. At the closing, I felt moved to put

Tim at the top of my list and I would find out a few years later how God had heard my prayers and those of others I'm sure, and spared Tim's life.

Kairos #3 proved to be yet another success. What I most remember about this particular weekend was walking into the prison for the closing and being met by this same inmate, Tim. He was one of the resident team members; these are inmates who have previously lived a Kairos weekend and are chosen through their own merit to come back to the next Kairos and be part of the team. Tim had made the team and was there to escort us across the yard. At OSR, the yard was open, meaning, the inmates were allowed to move about freely on the yard at designated times during the day. This was one of those times, as we made our way to the gym, amid many watchful and curious eyes. In the early days of Kairos, we would sometimes have 100 or more people attend a closing. After the closing, I found myself being one of the last to leave, and as I made my way back across the yard alone, Tim saw me and came to walk with me and say goodbye. He went with me, as far as the rules would allow, then he kind of leaned his head over so only I could hear and quietly said, "Please always pray for me, it's so hard to be a Christian in here." I assured him I would, always. As I left the gates, the fences, and razor wire that held Tim inside the walls, I prayed that he and countless others like him would always remember their true freedom, that freedom in Christ. Tim and I communicated through letters for a while, and through him, I learned something of the day-to-day struggles he faced, and what it is to live as an inmate in that environment. A couple years later I was driving in my car and praying my rosary. As I prayed for Tim, I was overcome with fear and such sadness that I had to pull over to the side of the road because I couldn't see to drive through the tears flooding my eyes. As I turned the engine off, I said, "Lord, I don't know what is wrong, I just know Tim is in some kind of danger and in dire need of you right now. In your mercy, please answer my prayer to come to Tim's aid in his time of desperate need of you." I continued praying on the rosary and after a while the sadness and tears disappeared and I was on my way again. Even though my tears for him subsided, the uneasiness and concern for his well being continued for a couple of days or more and I continued to plead for God's mercy for Tim.

As I entered the gym at another Kairos weekend closing, a few months later at Dick Connor Correctional Facility in Hominy, Oklahoma, we were once again excited to hear the testimonies of the men having just lived their Kairos weekend. As I got seated, Jean Key, a volunteer I had worked with from the beginning at Oklahoma State Prison and Oklahoma State Reformatory and whose husband Jim and she had contributed much time, talent, and labor to the success of Kairos in Oklahoma, tapped me on the shoulder and said, "Deanna, as you can see all the previous Kairos graduates have been allowed to attend this closing, and did you know Tim is sitting back there?" She went on to tell me she had learned that he had been in a terrible fight at Oklahoma State Reformatory and had been moved here to the Dick Connor Facility. She said she had heard that a couple of guys he owed money to had jumped him and beaten him pretty badly. As I went to say hello I was taken back by his appearance. He hardly looked like himself. He was badly bruised and still swollen from the broken bones and lacerations to his face due to the beating he had endured. He had undergone some plastic surgery as well. The closing was about to start and I told him I would visit with him again after the testimonies. As I was relating all this to my husband Jim, he said, he believed I needed to tell Tim about my prayer for him. In fact Jim insisted I tell Tim. When the closing was over and I began to relate my story of sadness and fear for his safety during my prayer, I could see he was overwhelmed and practically speechless. Tim and I visited some more and as we were ready to leave, he thanked me for my prayers and said he didn't know what to say. I told him he didn't have to say anything, to just praise God for His goodness.

The closing was on Sunday and on Wednesday I received a letter in the mail from Tim. Words did not escape him in the letter as they had Sunday night. He wrote 3 full pages and conveyed his emotions of that night to me in very expressive and sincere words. He began the letter by thanking me for my caring. He told me that after getting beaten he had lost his job that would have allowed him to get out of prison in a couple of years. He began turning his back on God because he couldn't understand why all this was happening to him. He said that when I told him I was praying at almost the exact time he was getting beaten, his mind started battling with his heart. He continued that what he saw on my face and heard coming from my mouth was genuine, caring, and thankfully his heart and God's Love won out. He said his heart started beating erratically, and God once more entered him. He continued in his letter telling me that when he returned to his cell later that night, God showed him that life is not eternal here on earth. That the day he was beaten down, the guards took him to a local hospital. On the way there he lost consciousness. He was told later, he had no vital signs upon arrival at the hospital. He said he didn't see any light at the end of a tunnel but when he was told, he was so very close to death, shivers ran up and down his spine. Shivers ran up and down again, he said, when I told him what happened when I was praying for him. He continued saying that it proved to him there is a God, how else could I have possibly felt so much dread and fear while praying for him and he believed my prayers were part of the reason God didn't take him then. However high his faith was lifted because of this encounter with God, mine was lifted equally as high.

We started going to Cimarron Correctional Facility in Cushing, Oklahoma. We go where we are needed and have served on many teams and many prisons over the years. I met an inmate named Mike for maybe the 2nd or 3rd time, but often it's as if I'm meeting these men and hearing their stories for the first time. I was inside the prison, in a room the inmate team uses to prepare snacks for those attending the weekend. I was keeping an eye on the brisket we had been warming in a roaster and talking with some of the inmate team. After a little while, most of the team left the room to tend to various duties. I had felt that Mike wanted to talk and I could sense that he was now going to take the opportunity. As he slowly pulled his chair over near me, he sat for maybe a minute or two without saying a word, then he opened the conversation by saying that everyone has a story, and wanted to know mine. I began by telling him of losing my mother at the age of 12 and being sent here to Oklahoma from my home in California to live with my sister at 16-years-old, got married at 16 and had my first son, Steve at 17. Then I had my second son Adam at the ripe old age of 20. I could have gone on a little bit talking about them, but I cut my story short knowing that Mike had a lot to say and these guys don't get a chance to talk to someone from the outside very often. So as I listened, he began by saying that we are all, "just a bunch of redeemed sinners", and he added, "some with tarnished halos." I've learned that in prison, you tell it like it is or at least as you perceive it to be. He continued his story by saying that he came from a good middle class family who provided well for him. These loving people adopted Mike at 3 months and let him know he was adopted at an appropriate age to understand. He said he had a good childhood, but things went horribly wrong when he was introduced to drugs at a very young age. By the young age of only seventeen, he was addicted to heroin and had killed a man. He was convicted of murder and received the death penalty, finding himself on death row at Oklahoma State Prison at McAlester, Oklahoma, and only just having turned eighteen. In 1976 Mike had been taken off death row, due to the decision by the powers that were at that time deeming the electric chair, used as the means of execution, inhumane treatment, as we had learned on my son's eight grade trip to Oklahoma State Prison.

Every inmate on death row was taken off and given life without parole. Mike was an inmate at McAlester the year my son and I were there in 1978, so when I told him I was writing about memories of my years as a Kairos volunteer, he offered to me information concerning his time spent there on death row. He talked about praying for God to send him a female companion, someone to share his life with, such as it was. He laughed as he told me one day he had a visitor and it turned out it was an Asian woman who related to him through very broken English that God had sent her to him. He said the incident made him a believer in prayer, but it could never have worked for him. They were worlds apart and it was not fair to her. Mike continued talking to me about his 50 years of life on this earth, 32 of which had been spent in prison. He talked a lot about his family and said he had always wondered why his birth mother had given him up for adoption. It happened that our conversation was just prior to the Sunday lunch dessert being served. The men attending the weekend sit with their table families and after they finish their meal, some of the resident team, bring in individual cakes iced and decorated with their names on them as the rest of us encircle them and sing "You are loved, you are beautiful. God danced the day you were born." This is one of the most moving and life changing moments in the weekend. Everything wraps up, not long after this lunch and although things are coming to an end, God sometimes saves the best for last, and so it was for Mike. Unlike him, most of the inmates aren't as fortunate by having been raised in a good home. Some, as small children and young adults, have been to hell and back. When all you learn and earn from your environment is hate, that's all you know to live and give. For more of them than my heart wants to believe, this may be the first time they have experienced any kind of love, and God's unconditional love is the means by which the walls they have built come tumbling down. Very often this is the first time they have received something and nothing was expected from them in return. This is not an excuse, but certainly a reason so many wind up behind bars. And so, as Mike expressed his desire to know why he was given up for adoption, I told him that speaking as a mother myself I could assure him of one thing: God gives mothers a deep and undying love for their children. Whatever gets in the way of feeling you are able to keep your child, it does not diminish the God given love, deep within the heart and soul of a mother for her child. And as I said to Mike, I would bet not only God but Mike's birth mother danced the day he was born.

I could see these words were moving Mike in a way only God can, as a sense of peace and healing filled the room and the hearts of Mike and these other children of God, as they gazed through tear-filled eyes, first at their cake, then at each other and their brothers and sisters in Christ. Hearts were being turned from stone to flesh, walls were coming down. For these who had come for many different reasons to see what Kairos was all about, they found their answer. Now they knew: Kairos is about love, God's love, a mother's love, a father's love, a friend's love. Only through Him are any of us able to show others a glimpse of that Love. As grace filled the room we were all shown much more than just a glimpse. From that moment, I came to the realization that more often than not, we can see much more clearly through tear-filled eyes. This moment of grace was heaven scented as we felt with our hearts, tasted with our mouths and saw with our eyes the sweet Glory of Our Savior, on each face. And to do this, he used, as Mike described all of us in that gym, redeemed sinners, some with tarnished halos and a piece of cake to bring it all about.

An incredible young man I met at Cimarron Correctional Facility was a member of a group called the brotherhood, much like the Aryan brotherhood that are for lack of a better term a hate group. J.D. was a leader in that group since coming to prison. As a child, he had been abused and that was a large factor that contributed to the bitterness he carried with him. Then through a Kairos weekend J.D. experienced God and love entered his heart totally changing him and literally saving his life. A life that was headed for destruction due to drugs and hate, which are some of Satan's weapons of choice. But through prayer and God's love, J.D. was transformed from a cold man of steel into a warm loving child of God. This is the J.D. I know today; the old J.D. has passed away. I think of St. Paul and how he was persecuting Christians, even having them killed, until he met Jesus and was struck by a blinding light and thrown off his horse. His life changed drastically that day and God used him powerfully to spread His Good news of salvation. So, when J.D. met Jesus through a Kairos weekend, you could say he was thrown off his horse, blinded by the light of Jesus' love and his life changed. He is an evangelizer, one who brings others to Jesus by their example of love, humility, and service. He is a joy to know and a testament to what God can do in our lives if we allow Him. I have witnessed him kneeling in prayer on concrete for hours at a time. He is in prayer for his brothers going through the weekend, praying for them to open their hearts to God.

J.D. had become friends with my husband Jim during the Kairos weekend and Jim had sort of "taken him under his wing" so to speak. J.D. confided in Jim and told him about a tattoo on the inside of his upper left arm that identified him as a leader in the brotherhood. During his Kairos weekend, he had such an amazing conversion he now detested all things to do with his past life of sin in the brotherhood. His tattoo, or "patch" as it was called, was a painful reminder and he felt he had to rid himself of it at any cost. And so he went to extreme measures to do so, which could have cost him the loss of his arm. One evening he made up his mind it was time and he took a pop-top lid off a can, heated it with the flame of a candle and began to burn and scrape the tattoo off his arm, leaving tender, raw and burnt flesh exposed. After months of pain from the initial process of removal, risk of infection, and the area having to receive debreeding procedures daily by the doctor and nurses, his arm finally healed. When I asked him how he endured that much pain he said he thought of the pain Christ had to endure to save his soul and in comparison to Christ's pain, his was nothing.

CHAPTER VI

A Man Named Josiah

Horizon at Davis Correctional Facility in Holdenville Oklahoma is a ten-month program following the four-day Kairos weekend. Davis is the only facility I know of in the state where Kairos allows groups other than Christians to attend the Kairos four-day weekend. Muslims, American Indians, Jews, and wiccans are all allowed to attend the Kairos weekend. They have their own areas and have their own teachings, but are welcome to join in our activities as well. With the exception of the wiccans who practice paganism, magic, and witchcraft, the other religions have some similar beliefs with Christians.

I began going to Davis Correctional Facility in 2006 on Tuesday nights with four other volunteers. The classes were geared toward teaching coping skills to the inmates. Coping with prison life, separation from family, friends, society as a whole, anger management, and parenting skills. The inmates were taught about the effects of drug and alcohol abuse and the dangers and evil of abuse of any kind. The majority of the men were a living witness to the effects. The classes were presented by volunteers and staff, and so

I knew my being asked to lead one was just a matter of time. When my time came, I was asked to give the class on parenting. I knew I had to rely on God and as expected, everything went well. We met in the Horizon unit in which they were housed and I remember the first time I walked in being amazed at the quiet and calm inside. There were two floors with 25 cells upstairs and 25 downstairs, and 2 men to a cell making a total of 100 inmates in the unit. The men upstairs had already been through the program and at the end of this one would be moved to another unit on the yard. Those going through the program at this time would be moved upstairs when finished.

Being sentenced to prison can be a wake up call for some. It is the reality of the choices we make in life. Many had lost their families, friends, hope of once again holding a decent job, things that didn't make the top of their list on the outside, but they were now faced with the reality of the wrong choices they had made. For some, a wake up call, a time for change, of getting better, of knowing they don't have to return to a life of drugs and crime once they are released. For others, it is just a chance to hit the snooze button again, take another five minutes, a time out, and then continue on the road that is most familiar to them, that road that leads them back to a life of drugs, crimes of all sorts and back to exactly what got them locked up to start with. Unfortunately for some, it's the only road they know. As Kairos's volunteers, we were there to follow the

Kairos motto, "Listen, Listen, Love, Love," and help them learn some skills to better handle the situations in which they may find themselves, on a daily basis. As Christians, we tried to be witnesses of faith, hope, and love, and as Christ tells us, the greatest of these is love. We were there to bring Christ's light into the darkness, to give them the knowledge of salvation and eternal life and the assurance that there were those of us willing to walk the journey with them.

On my Kairos journey I've met some very interesting people along the way. Some very spiritual people as well as some with what I consider odd or at least different beliefs. Many I believe to be sincerely searching for peace, happiness, something that will make sense of the crazy world in which they live, called prison. At Davis Correctional Facility we sat at tables of around six inmates and one or two volunteers. After spending time together once a week for 10 months the inmates got to know me and knew they could trust me. Trust doesn't come easy for them. I was treated with respect and I felt at ease with them, yet never letting myself forget or be naïve about the environment into which God had called me. I learned that if God calls you to do something out of your comfort zone, you can be assured He will give you the ability to achieve the goal. Leaving your comfort zone only makes you stronger. Saying that they knew they could trust me may sound odd, but trust is a sacred commodity inside the prison. I prayed that if they saw they could trust in me, this would bring them one step closer to trust God, the Spirit. After all, the Spirit of God within us was what we were bringing to them.

We shared with them that there will always be struggles, that we on the outside struggle, but it was possible to live the life God intended for them if they would trust God, to let Him change their way of thinking and looking at the world and believe that there are those of us who care about them. By the witness of our lives to them we show them that anyone can change if they want to and will trust God to help them.

Two years later, I started going to Davis Correctional Facility on Monday night rather than Tuesdays. It was quite a bit different because Mondays weren't really structured but simply a time for visiting, and this could involve playing board games, cards, dominoes, watching videos or just talking. You can come to know a lot about a person if you're a good listener and the person is telling you the truth. In prison, you can also be hearing a total fabrication told to you for a variety of reasons, not the least of which is the con game. I sat with the Muslims and did a lot of listening to a man named Josiah. He was an African American, who had converted to Islam. This conversion to Islam is common among African Americans in prison. Some white inmates join the Aryans, a lot of Latinos join gangs who often have division among themselves, just as they did on the outside. North against South, turf against turf. Some

American Indians join together and learn their traditional ways, the ways of their ancestors. You have to belong to something in that kind of environment, because it is tough and can be dangerous to go it alone. Being a Christian, and being a member of the Christian faith is not a choice that is voluntarily made by most inmates. Because Christians are looked upon as weak and it most often takes a profound experience of, or a profound encounter with Christ to soften their hearts of stone, so that they can start living the lives God intended for them.

Like I said earlier, I spent a lot of time listening to Josiah. He was a small man in stature and was always neatly dressed in his prison khakis and would bring his prayer shawl with him from time to time. It was a beautifully woven piece almost like a rug, heavy and thick with many bright colors, and I could tell he was very proud of it. Josiah was, for lack of a better word, interesting. He liked talking about his faith, and so I listened, and I think I learned about not only the Muslim religion as Josiah understood it, but I also learned a lot about Josiah as well. His story went that he had been raised in the midst of drugs, alcohol, prostitution, and crimes of all kinds. He told me that within his family, pimping was a family business. As he showed me the scar from a bullet wound to the head, he said that it had been put there by the hand of his own father. But he believed he had survived because God had a purpose for his life, to stop the cycle of crime and violence in his family. Well, it sounded like a story that could be possible and that you might hear in prison, but you learn to realize, it may or may not be true. I found out a few months later that Josiah had another story about his upbringing and family that was quite different from the one I was told. One night another volunteer and I started talking and I learned Josiah had given her a story of him being raised in a very strict religious home, with his father being a pastor. Which story is true? We don't know and it doesn't matter because we're here to "Listen, Listen, Love, Love."

At some point, Josiah decided that he would be my mentor and Spiritual guide. You see, I later found out that Josiah thought himself to be a prophet. For that very reason, he began telling me things about my childhood that, in his words, "only a prophet could know." Most of his assumptions and ideas were so off base, it was as if you were at a carnival and had just entered the palm readers/magicians tent. Sometimes, the visits got so serious, that it was taking the joy out of going and ministering to those at the prison. Try as I might I couldn't convince him that everything in my life was going just fine. The final straw came when I asked Josiah how he was doing, one Tuesday night. He said he was fine and asked how my past week had been. "Great", I said, "everything's going great." With that, he kind of squinted his eyes and in a very doubt filled voice said, "are you sure you're okay?" "Yes," I replied, but nothing I said could convince him that I was happy and well.

You see, Josiah wanted to do a little more palm reading and magic tricks that night, but I knew I had to do something. I wasn't there to play those kinds of games, so I simply prayed for God to release me from that situation. I had wanted Josiah to see that I was a joyful person, because of my relationship with Christ, but Josiah only wanted to see what he wanted to see. I have often been asked, "How do you know if you're being conned?" The answer to that question is, you don't. It doesn't matter. As Kairos volunteers, we are to follow the rules of the Department of Corrections and the rules of Kairos. We are not allowed to bring anything into the prison, and we can't take anything out, we can't do any favors for anyone, even someone you may think you could trust, so being conned is really something you don't want to have happen, but it is a non issue if you follow the rules. As a Christian, the mission is to be present to them, show them Christ's Love and pray it changes their hearts so that they may live with Him in eternity. So the only one losing is the one running the con.

God answered my prayer and Josiah suddenly became very distant with me, very disinterested. He eventually joined the Jewish group and told me he had really found where he belonged. I told him I was happy for him and I continue to pray he will someday have a relationship with Jesus. Josiah is searching, and that in itself is a very good thing. Scripture tell us that Jesus' parents couldn't find him for 3 days, they searched for Him and on the 3rd day found him in the temple, Christ always lets Himself be found, all we have to do is open our eyes and our hearts and we will realize that He was always visible, always reachable and always lovingly and patiently waiting for our return. I am reminded of a joke I heard about a priest on a train bound for Chicago who was reading a newspaper while a young evangelical was thumbing through a well-worn Bible. Unable to hold himself quiet any longer the young evangelical said to the priest, "Have you found Jesus?" The priest lowering his newspaper looked at the young man and said, "Is he lost again?"

CHAPTER VII

Love Etched Into Leather

I next began sitting with the American Indians, because there weren't enough volunteers and no one was with them. I immediately felt at ease, and for whatever reason, they as well, were very comfortable with me joining their group. Leading and teaching this group is a man named Cainey and whose Indian name means Red Wolf Walking. He is a full blood Creek Indian, a medicine man and the leader and teacher of the traditional Indian religion and ways. He tries to help bring the younger men who have Indian blood in them back to their roots, of which many know nothing of their rich heritage. He believes through his teachings they will find their identity, who they are, and ultimately, who they can become as creations of the Creator, God. When I saw Cainey for the first time, he could have just stepped out of a traditional American Indian painting. His skin is dark and smooth, with very few lines on his face for a man of 60 years. He has long, black hair sprinkled with a few silver ones. It is usually pulled back at the nape of his neck and kept there with a band. His facial features are broad but not too broad, and his black eyes reveal a man who has lived a

full life, even though a portion of it has been behind concrete walls and layers of razor wire. He was an officer in the
army, he has a supportive family, several children and many
grandchildren and a contagious sense of humor. When he
talks about his newest grandchild Zach, you can feel the
love he has for him and how much he desires to be a part
of Zach's life, even if it is from behind prison walls. Zach's
grandmother brings Zach to the prison, on days of visitation as often as she can. Cainey has many gifts and one he
is very skilled at is working with leather. He has donated
his time and talent to charity work and recently took me to
the leather shop to show me a beautiful pair of moccasins
he had made for Zach. He next moved to the back corner
of the shop where on a shelf sat a small saddle with hand
carved designs of flowers and leaves and other very intri-
cate designs.

As I looked at this precious gift for Zach, I saw more
than just a gift for his grandson, from a master craftsman. I
saw the tremendous amount of love that was in every turn
of every cut that was made in the leather. The leather was
sacred as he etched and carved his very heart and soul into
the making of it. It made me realize how we are much like
the leather. Without God we are plain and without purpose
or meaning, but if we let him have our wills let him carve
and etch into us, his very heart he can turn us into a beautiful gift for others. And even though I know Cainey must
have regrets, as many of us do, I also know the hope and

peace that fills him. He is a recovered alcoholic who suffers from the pain of arthritis, having been thrown off too many bulls as a young bull rider, he told me. When he feels he has done well spiritually, he rewards himself by wearing his hair in braids wrapped in leather bands. It seems he has made the best of his time served in prison. He is following the "Red Road" which is a metaphor for living within the Creator's rules. Living a life of truth, friendship, respect, spirituality and humanitarianism.

After getting to know us and becoming our friends, Cainey asked my husband Jim and I if we would be sponsors for the American Indians at Davis Correctional Facility. We told him we would be happy to, but that we weren't sure we knew what all that entailed. He said it basically meant that we would be able to bring in the medicines used in the Sweat Lodge Ceremonies. The sweats are a sacred part of American Indian religion. There are required days of fasting beforehand and the heat and different herbs and medicines are used to purify both mind and body by sweating out the toxins and impurities within us. A good healthy meal is to be eaten afterward to replenish your strength, but that is rarely available in prison. Often times it only means maybe an extra slice of cheese or bread. I believe Cainey's teaching practices are effective because I have seen the fruits in him and those he is teaching. The American Indians who have gone through a Kairos weekend and the Horizon program are the only group who, of those released from prison, have not returned. A lot of what they are learning is what we learn as Christians, but they don't openly acknowledge Jesus as the author of their teachings. A big part of that is that when they come to prison, it's just not real popular to say you're a Christian. But the truth is, a lot of times it's not very popular to say you're Indian, either. Throughout history, they have been made to believe they must give up every bit of their culture, who they are, and become what a particular group perceived Christianity to be. It is still happening today. As Christians, our work is to be Christ's hands and feet, reaching out in gentleness and love to all God's children, welcoming and inviting them to love Him because He first loved us. He doesn't want to strip us of our very being, but rather mold and shape us into His being, His image. Of course we all have free will to accept or reject Christ's Love, but how will they know this Love if we don't show them? And how can we show them, if we ourselves have not let Him mold and shape us? So, as I interact and even connect in many ways through most strongly our humor but also our interests, I am learning about Indian ways and they are learning about Christ's love for all His children. And so, I have Faith that I am doing the will of God, I have Hope that I am helping to further the Kingdom and bringing Christ's Love to those who are in need of His Love, and as Scripture tells us, "the greatest of these is Love."

We arrived at the Davis Correctional Facility, on the first Monday of the month and went to the inmates unit instead of meeting with them in the visitation room. It was time for count and so they were in their house. You never know how long count will last, so there was nothing we could do but wait. We sat in our usual places, Jim at his group's table and me in the far northeast corner of the unit, under a big sign painted high on the wall of the upper story, that reads, " American Indians Circle of Nations" and another that says "All My Relations." As I read the sign, I felt a sense of what it is to be proud of who you are and to what you belong. As a child, I had always heard the whisperings within my family, about an Indian grandmother on my mother's side of the family. Yet no one talked openly about her, as if there was something of which to be ashamed. But I was always curious and so a few years ago I started to try to find out about this woman, my great grandmother. Most of the elder generation in my family has passed away, except for one 92 year old, aunt Babe, who was still living and in sound health of mind and body. So, she and the Internet became my source of information. I learned that Sarah Jane Hunt, a Choctaw Indian woman removed from her home in Mississippi and forced to travel by foot to Oklahoma, on the appropriately named "Trail of Tears," was my dear great-grandmother. As I waited for count to clear, I thought of her, how we are all connected, and if we look for this truth, this connection, we will find it. As I sat there, I could almost feel her presence. I was proud of the heritage she had given me and most importantly, I was grateful to her and what she must have had to endure. I felt very connected to her.

Suddenly, count was over and all fifty-cell doors opened at the same time. I was greeted first by Cainey as he and his cellmate emerged. He was at first apologetic for the wait, and at the same time, he seemed very rushed as he told me in hurried words that tonight would be a little different than usual. He told me that Jim and I were in for a surprise and I could not imagine what it could be. As the inmates and volunteers visited as usual, downstairs Cainey instructed a tall slender young man named Tommy to escort me upstairs amid curious eyes. He is nice looking, and well mannered, very intelligent as well as having a charming personality. What in the world were people like Tommy and Cainey doing in a place like this? The answer is drugs and alcohol, and statistics show that 85% of crimes are drug related. "I have never been to the second floor," I said to Tommy as we climbed to the top of the stairs. "Well," he said, "this is where we bring all our dates" and we both laughed. I also said a little silent prayer for the gift of laughter. He then opened a door for me that led to a very small room and every inch of the room was taken up by tables and chairs arranged in a square. To our surprise, there they were, all the men that Jim and I visit with each Monday night. A young man named Jerry, who had been a cook and who was in Jim's group, had gotten together with Cainey, and they had decided to make us a dinner. They had gotten the go-ahead from the chaplain and their unit manager and they were so excited.

In a moment, in walked Jerry with a three gallon plastic bucket, filled with rice that smelled and tasted delicious. "When was the last time you ate rice out of a three gallon bucket with a bunch of prisoners?" He asked as we all laughed. Next, Cainey entered with arms loaded down with tortilla chips, jalapeno peppers, picante sauce, soy sauce and other condiments to go with the rice. The rice was also full of bell peppers, onions, sausage and all kinds of spices. Just as that unlikely mixture of ingredients, can be turned into a delicious meal. So too can an unlikely mixture of people, in a tiny room on a Monday night in the hands of God, come to know who they are and feel what it is to belong. For some, this was the first time they had experienced what it is to gather round the dinner table, eat, laugh, and share as family. Before the meal, Jerry had led the blessing. He thanked God for the food, for friends like us and for allowing us to have this dinner at all, which is a rare occasion in this environment. As he ended his blessing, he asked God's forgiveness for the items they had stolen from the kitchen to make this dinner possible. We all laughed and said, "Amen."

CHAPTER VIII

The Smoke Off

We met this Monday night inside the visitation room. There was only enough space for a table, seven chairs, and just enough room to get into your chair and out again. I found something that aroused my curiosity about this particular room we would be meeting in for the next 10 months. It locks from the inside. When someone comes to the door, one of us must open it before they can come in. This reminded me of a picture used during one of the Kairos talks called "Opening the Door." It is a picture of Jesus standing in front of a door knocking, and there's no doorknob on the outside of the door. Someone must open it before He can come in. He doesn't force His way into our hearts, but gently knocks, hoping we will let Him in. As I entered, I was met at the door by Cainey and the sound of Indian flutes and drums. Cainey had brought a CD player, and the music was very welcoming as I found my place at the table. This was a new group of men I had only met once and three or four of them were very quiet, but this wasn't surprising since we did not yet know each other. As the night wore on, they seemed to be relaxing a little bit. I tried to be very low key and just follow Cainey's lead until they got to know me and I them. As I listened to their stories of growing up Indian and poor, I not only learned something about each one as an individual, but also the importance of powwows, music, singing, and family in the life of the American Indian. The rhythmic beating of the drums and almost lonesome sound of the flute was a beautiful accompaniment to the sharing of their lives with us all.

A young man named William, only twenty-two years of age, was studying out of an English to Creek language dictionary. He appeared to be the most serious of the group, which may be because of his age, as everyone else had at least fifteen years on him and he has trouble relating to some of the stories being told. I was looking forward to hearing his story as the 10 months progressed. Cainey had brought some jokes and anecdotes that he read to us, along with the laughter I knew God would use to bind our spirits together.

I asked about anything that was needed for the sweat lodge, such as sweet grass, tobacco, flat cedar or sage. This got them wondering and asking me if I could make some of the traditional dishes they grew up eating such as sofkia, fry bread, meat pies, etc. I told them I could cook just about anything, that I make meat pies, especially around Mardi Gras time, for my kids and grandkids, and I've made fry bread as well. I told them I would ask the chaplain to give me the okay to bring some food in for them. As I didn't want to get their hopes up too high in case my request was denied, I added that I wasn't sure how the fry bread and meat pies would taste by the time they traveled from my home in Norman to theirs in Holdenville, about an hour and a half drive. Then, as if with just one voice, they all answered, "delicious."

We are meeting down in the unit for the rest of the program due to the visitation room being used by another group. I met with the guys upstairs in the TV room, the same room we had the rice dinner in last year. As I walked in this particular Monday night, I sensed a different mood. A more somber and serious feeling filled the room. As I took my place at the table and looked at Billy sitting directly across from me working on a crossword puzzle, I noticed his long dark braided hair that almost reached his waist had been cut short above his shoulders. Knowing that cutting your hair was sometimes a sign of mourning for those who keep to the traditional Indian ways, I asked what had happened, and he told me his mother had died on Saturday. I gave him my condolences and this opened the door for him to speak of how he needed to talk to his aunts, her sisters, and be a better nephew. He recalled memories of his childhood growing up poor and Indian, but even though they didn't have much they were happy times, he recounted. After a few minutes, he resumed working his crossword puzzle and didn't say much the rest of the night.

We arrived a little late this Monday night and when we got to the unit the program was underway as I climbed the stairs to the TV room. After our greeting each other, I listened to Cainey talk about his grandson Zach, the apple of his eye.

I told him that my granddaughters Danielle, Ashley, and Cayla were doing great and as we continued talking, I noticed a small package lying in front of him. My curiosity got the best of me and I asked him what it was. He replied that it was medicines, sweetgrass, tobacco, cedar, and sage, and that we were going to have a smoke off tonight. I had seen them smoking off before from a distance during a four-day Kairos weekend, but until now I had not had the opportunity to be a part of it. Cainey opened a box of matches that contained only one lone match. He said he felt a little bit like Barney Fife whom Sheriff Andy Taylor would allow to have only one bullet for his gun and Barney had to keep it in his shirt pocket. Cainey began by lighting a candle that ignited some tissue resting on top, which in turn kindled the smudge stick that has the medicines secured by string and formed into a cigar shape. As the smoke filled the room I was filled with thanksgiving to God for this sacred moment. The smoke reminded me a little bit like during Mass when the priest incenses the altar, the lectionary, or the people, symbolizing our prayers rising to God. During a smoke off the medicine man purifies himself, the air around him, and then the participants do the same, passing the smoke over their bodies so that our prayers rise up to the Creator. Cainey stood in front of me, passed the smoke over me as he prayed in his Creek language for blessings for me. I was moved and felt God's Spirit with us.

CHAPTER IX

A Calling

I arrived at Davis Correctional Facility around 6:25p.m. and after going through the process of signing in, giving the correctional officer my ID badge, receiving a visitors badge in return, taking off my earrings, rings, shoes and jacket and passing them through the detector, much like those used in airports, I walked through the larger metal detector myself. Having passed with no buzzers going off, I proceeded to put the items back on, and was then ready to go across the prison yard to the Kairos unit named Charlie South. Procedures and rules change suddenly within the prison system from day to day sometimes, and this was one of those days. A week ago you had to be escorted by a correctional officer across the yard. It was different tonight because you could go across on your own.

The other volunteers were already down on the unit and Jim hadn't come with me tonight. I pushed the button on the door that would lead me down the hall to another door that opened out onto the yard, took a deep breath, and walked into the world of those behind the walls. Six o'clock until seven or so is chow time and there is a lot of movement on the yard with inmates going to and coming from the chow hall. I was right in the middle of it. I wouldn't say I was afraid because I had been on the yard many times before. But for two years or more I had gotten used to having an escort and so I felt conspicuous and a little uncomfortable making my way to Charlie South Unit alone. So, I said a little silent prayer for an angel to be with me and help me not feel so uncomfortable on my walk to the unit. Suddenly, beside me walked a Kairos graduate from a couple of years ago. He was a man you could only describe as "a mountain of a man." He was around 50+ years of age, worn from this life he was living, and looked older than he actually was. His gray hair, shoulder length but clean, fell over one eye and across his cheek. "Can I escort you to Charlie South?" he said. He didn't say much more after I happily answered, "yes." Then as I turned to my left, I was joined by William, the young Creek man in our group, asking me if I would like some company, since we were both going to the same unit. Again, I gladly said "yes" and thanked them both. I not only thanked God for answering my prayer, but for letting me realize that angels don't always have wings and halos, but that He uses all his children to help us along our journey. Later that evening, this same young man, so quiet and shy, said he had a message to give me before I left. And so as we were leaving, he walked up to me, shook my hand, and with eyes as black as the midnight sky looking deep into mine, said in his native Creek language, "The lady wearing green tonight has a very good heart." I knew at that moment that he trusted me and I was to hear his story soon. We all have a story to tell and often times we just need to find that someone who will listen and never judge us, knowing the good and the bad, and still love us, someone you can not only call a friend, but who also becomes a part of your story.

All prisons in Oklahoma have been locked down since before Thanksgiving 2009 due to simultaneous fights breaking out in 5 or 6 of the state's prisons. It seems to have been a racially fueled battle. As of March 1, 2010, Davis Correctional Facility is still on lockdown. Several attempts have been made to loosen the restrictions on the inmates but all to no avail, because as soon as they give them some freedom, problems arise and once more they are locked down. We were to have our 4-day weekend March 8-11, but it was moved to some time in April. I'm sure those who have had no part in all of the problems are getting very discouraged and so many prayers are being said for peace to come to all involved

We are going forward with our plans for the four-day, as usual. I am trying to find a store to buy my crawfish to make etouffee for the team. I will also be making a trip to Marlow, Oklahoma to buy one hundred and twenty pounds of taco meat to make taco salads for the inmates. I will have plenty of help from Danielle, Ashley, and Cayla as they love to cook and are excellent help. We always have so much fun together. What blessings they are.

I have come to realize the spiritual benefits that I have been missing these few months by not being able to visit the inmates. You would imagine that it is a one sided coin and that you visit those in prison to give something whether it's your time, your talents and your love for God and neighbor, and this is surely true, but the other side of it is that you get something in return. Something so beautiful, so fulfilling and right, it has to be in God's plan for your life. I believe we all have a calling. I also believe we can have many callings throughout our lives and one of the greatest gifts is to know to what we have been called, and to be able to answer that call, no matter how difficult or how far from what you may have thought your calling to be. I believe I am here to be the best wife, mother, grandmother, aunt, sister, cousin, friend, and person I can be by letting others see Christ's Love for them through me. And I am certain there are times when I fail, but I know also that I am expected to keep trying. I also know that I am called to visit the prisoner, to set the captive free by letting them see Christ's Love for them through me. And so I lift my voice to sing your praises, Lord. Thank you for my calling.

We received a letter from an inmate named Johnny whom we've known for many years, who had been transferred from Cimarron Correctional Facility to Joseph Harp. He was in good spirits and said although he will miss seeing us, he knows this is God's will for him. He is mentoring some of the younger men and trying to guide them to the path Johnny himself is on now. This path is the road less traveled, the narrow road as the Bible calls it, and among traditional American Indians, it is the "red road." No matter what name we choose it is the road that leads to Eternal Life through Christ Jesus. It is encouraging to hear from those we have met over the years and find out they are doing well.

CHAPTER X

Cell #170

I just finished reading a book titled *Prison Writings* by Leonard Peltier and it has stirred my soul. The preface of the book is written by Ramsey Clark, counsel to Leonard Peltier, and former Attorney General of the United States. Leonard is an American Indian imprisoned for the last thirty-two years and whom I believe, along with a multitude of others, is unjustly accused. In Ramsey Clark's preface, he says he thinks he can explain beyond a doubt that Leonard has committed no crime. There is absolutely no evidence that he killed anyone. All the evidence against him was utterly misleading and fabricated circumstantial evidence. He says that even if he had been guilty of firing the gun that killed two FBI agents, and it is certain that he did not, it would still have been in self-defense. It would have been in defense not just of his people but of the right of all individuals and peoples to be free from domination and exploitation. He continues that the 1970's were a time of government paranoia against all dissident groups that remained as the Vietnam War era was drawing to a close. On Pine Ridge

Reservation, South Dakota, in 1975 that paranoia was evident as the United States Marshall's office laid siege. It was a bloody conflict, the likes of which had not been seen since the Civil War. Leonard has chosen the high road, by making the best of his time served in prison, as has our friend, Cainey and J.D. He mentors other inmates, reads avidly, studies law books, and probably has more knowledge of the law than those who make it their livelihood. He has become "freer than his captors," as one review of the book puts it. He says his only crime is being Indian and in some small way I understand, because being a Catholic in Oklahoma, I have felt the prejudice of those who are ignorant of the Catholic Church and its teachings. As a sponsor and being part of the Native American Indian group at the prison, I have felt the prejudice from other volunteers, some of whom are quick to let you know they are Christian. I believe their prejudice comes to them through their ignorance and unwillingness to learn about others. Also a lack of security in their own beliefs hinder them from realizing we are all God's children and we are called to love one another. Through that love we can learn from each other and find out that we are not all that different from one another; after all there is only one true God, the source of our love for others is Christ and it comes from Christ's love for us. That love can win hearts and set our spirits free by letting us see each other more clearly. It can change our lives and give us a yearning deep inside to have more of this love, which is Christ himself. We are all God's children whether we make the sign of the cross, pray in the Creek language, or know all the books of the Bible by heart. Mahatma Ghandi made the statement that he would have considered becoming Christian if he had ever met one living their faith.

I am looking forward to our next visit to Davis Correctional Facility and to discuss the book with my Indian brothers and to hear their impression and insight into the writings of Leonard Peltier and I am confident they are aware of the book, even if they haven't read it. I'm sure Cainey has, as he is very well read on all things Indian.

It has been weeks now, since we have been to Davis Correctional Facility because of the lockdown. We have worked three Kairos weekends in a row at Davis Correctional Facility in October, two weeks later at Cimarron Correctional Facility, and two weeks later at James Crabtree Correctional Center in Helena, Oklahoma. This proved to be a bit much for me as I had a rib cap come out of place in my back. After several visits to the chiropractor and a fair amount of pain, it is finally healing, but not without another problem cropping up. It seems I tore the cartilage in my knee, as well. I was determined not to go to the doctor and have test after test done, just so they could tell me I had somehow messed up my knee. I already knew that and I also believe that your body can heal itself if we have the time to rest and allow it to do so. And that is what I have done and I am getting better every day. Thanksgiving, Christmas, and New Years came and went and through it all, I rested my knee. Although we haven't been to Davis Correctional Facility since October.

The Wednesday after New Years day on Saturday, we headed for Davis Correctional Facility as it was up and running again. We arrived at about 6:15 to Unit D and they were having count. It had changed from eight o'clock to six o'clock now. Things are always changing in the prison system and you have to be patient and changeable as well. We had a relatively short wait and the program for the night could proceed. Because of the cartilage damage to my knee, I could not make the climb up the stairs to the T.V. room where we usually meet. So I told the chaplain and he talked to Cainey and decided I could meet with them in one of their cells, their "house" as it is commonly referred to. At first I thought he was making a joke, but then in all seriousness he said we could meet in one of the guy's cells. He had cleared it with the powers that be and all was well. This was another first for me. There we sat, in cell #170, seven Indian men and me, all of us ranging from twenty-five to sixty-eight years of age.

The youngest, twenty-five year old Nathan, is blond and blue eyed, yet has the facial features of his Cherokee tribe, of which he is very proud. As the eldest of the group, Bear as he is known, has much wisdom and chooses to share it neatly tucked inside his almost dry sense of humor. Bear had signed up for the program many times and then would back out because he didn't think he had much to offer to the group, but his offering turned out to be quite the opposite A most interesting fact about Bear is that he is the great grandson of the Chiricahua Apache leader Geronimo. Geronimo was born in 1829 and died in 1909 at Fort Sill, Oklahoma. If you have ever seen pictures of Geronimo and could see Bear, there is a definite family resemblance. He says he has many stories about Geronimo that have been passed down to his mother then to him and I am hoping I get to hear some of them.

Many years ago, I went to see *Geronimo* the movie, starring Wes Studi, a Cherokee from Tahlequah, Oklahoma, in the title role. I distinctly remember how sad I felt at the treatment of not only Geronimo, but of his people, our brothers and sisters, our fellow human beings. I recall having so much empathy for them that I cried and cried and my husband, who was also moved by the plight of Geronimo and his people were saddened by man's inhumanity to man, as well."

"Are we the only ones in the theater moved by this?" I asked him. "Surely not, but for some reason it seems to have gotten to us in a very profound way," was his reply to my question. So, here I am years later, crammed into a tiny eight-by-six cell #170, preparing for a smoke off with Geronimo's great grandson. I could never have imagined as a young woman, that in my early 60's, on a cold Wednesday night in January, this is where I would be and this is what I'd be doing. At first the only empty chair was right next to the urinal or toilet. Cainey, noticing this, asked the man whose cell we were in to move my chair two places over. In a space that small, I was still right next to the toilet. A young inmate named Jason told me a few years ago, "we live in a bathroom." Now I know what he meant. The cells are 8 feet long and 6 feet wide. The only furnishings in them are the bunk beds, made of steel and attached to the concrete wall, and the only way to get to the top bunk is by way of a kind of notch, just big enough to get a foothold in the metal rail to help hoist your self upon the mattress, that is only about 2 inches thick. It is hardly enough to keep the cold metal from going through and chilling you to the very bone, especially on a cold winter night in January in Oklahoma. But, such is life in prison. One of the elders named Sage led the night's meeting and did a great job of teaching the younger ones about how to live according to the Indian ways. He told them not to try to learn the ways too fast because you might miss something. Pray always and make every thing a prayer. Pray with and for others and the Creator will be there in your midst, because He promised, where two or more are gathered, there will I be also. Cainey is teaching Sage to be a leader, so that the circle of knowledge and ways continue down through the generations to come. Many times after sharing one of my experiences with someone, an experience such as sitting in a cell with seven of my Indian brothers, I've been asked, "Aren't you afraid?" My answer is always no, because first of all I know I'm there because this is God's plan for me and second the peace I have in this type of situation is from Him. How else could I explain to anyone that on any Wednesday night, without God, this is where I would be spending my evenings. But because I am sure God is directing it all, I look forward to and anticipate Wednesday nights with great joy and peace, the peace that passes all understanding and I have come to love these brothers with a holy love.

It was another Wednesday night at Davis Correctional Facility in Holdenville, but this time we met in the television room where they are allowed to watch videos and certain shows. My knee was healing and so I was able to climb the stairs, although slowly. We started the meetings with prayer and then a smoke off to purify our surroundings and offer our prayers to God. We use the meditation book Cainey authored, as a guide for our discussions. Tonight we shared that keeping God at the center of our being is the way to healing in every area of our life. Bear was the only one absent, so I will offer prayers for him and hopefully he can join us next week. Every one shared their thoughts and feelings on the night's subject and most in the group seem open to say what is on their mind and heart. Sage said last week, in his teaching, that speaking what the Creator gives you, to speak, may help someone in the group. He said that failing to do so robs not only the other person of a blessing, but yourself as well. All in all it was a good night of sharing. Afterward, we talked about maybe having a night where the volunteers bring in food like hamburgers and hot dogs. Then Cainey asked me an odd question: "How good is your throwing arm?" Immediately I knew it would be something funny, I just didn't know exactly what. "Why?" I asked suspiciously. "Oh, we were just wondering if you could make us some fry bread with a pork chop stuffed inside and get it over the razor wire, or better yet just wear a big coat and bring it in with you next Wednesday night." We all laughed and laughed, as I told them it would definitely be their last meal, at least from me. Once again I see the effect that humor has on both them and me and what a gift it is to us as I hear, see, and feel God use it to bind us together and bring healing.

Fry bread is a staple in the American Indian diet, just as tortillas are for the Mexican people and baguettes are for the French. I have realized through hearing stories of home and family, of that yearning for fry bread, that it is also a yearning for home and family, even if their younger years and upbringing were not ideal. For others, their childhoods were happy, they had loving parents and they have good memories. Even though fry bread is not physically the healthiest food they could be eating, neither is the food they serve them on a daily basis in the prison. But maybe fry bread can be healthy for them, both spiritually and emotionally. So as I prepare food for them, I will pray God uses it to take them back to a wholesome place in their lives, that He will give them a yearning for the Goodness He has prepared for them, from the beginning. I can say with conviction that I know Cainey has that yearning and knows that Goodness is God. And so, I will pray that they all come to understand Jesus in a different way than has been presented to them in the past, perhaps. Well-meaning Christians sometimes get it wrong. These men behind prison walls, whom I call my friends, need to know that. If we are ever to let anyone see the Loving Jesus through us, we have to get rid of the "spiritual bad breath" that does nothing to further the Kingdom. As Christians, we need to be careful of how we introduce Jesus to others. We need to make sure our breath is sweet and our words are His. In the Bible, the book of Jeremiah, chapter 15 verse 19, says that Jeremiah was so distraught trying to bring people to God with no success that, he was considered a man of strife and contention by everyone. He was so distraught he even came to the point of saying, "Woe to me, mother that you gave me birth." Then the Lord said to him, "If you repent so that I restore you, in My Presence you shall stand. If you bring forth the precious without the vile, you shall be my mouthpiece. Then it shall be they who turn to you." You may be the only Bible some people ever read. We must be the channels, the instruments through which Jesus' light shines, the Light that will guide our souls through whatever darkness we have experienced into the Light of His Love. Through Grace we are saved, through faith we are being saved and through works others will see the peace and joy He gives and come to believe in Him who died and brings salvation for us all, because as Scripture says, "Faith without works is dead." I want my faith to be a living faith. And this is the reason I do what I do.

CHAPTER XI

Worthy of Love

Recently I cooked for a Kairos weekend at Cimarron Correctional Facility in Cushing Oklahoma. It will probably be the last time I work a weekend in the role of food manager as it is getting physically too hard for me. I have accepted a position on the state advisory council of Oklahoma as Food Coordinator, which is basically what I've been doing all along, without the physical work now. After 17 years I now have an official title. It makes me laugh but in a good way. On that weekend I heard a joke from another volunteer, whom I have grown to adore, Pat O'Kelly who can put a smile on everyone's face. The joke goes like this: A man named George goes to heaven and is telling Saint Peter about all these acquaintances of his and how horrible a life they lived and how there is no way they should be allowed into heaven. Joe went out on his wife all the time. Tom was the biggest liar in the world; he would lie to his own grandmother. Bill was caught stealing money from the bank where he was the vice president and Ted was the worst of all he thought because he was seen at the local bar every Friday night smoking, drinking, cussing, and in the company of the not-so-reputable women of the town. Then would show up at church Sunday morning, as if he were a saint. No it just wouldn't be right for them to go to heaven. Later, Saint Peter was showing him around heaven when they came to a room and there sat Tom, Joe, Bill and Ted, with their mouths gaped open and a look of sheer confusion on their faces. What in the world happened to these guys and why do they look like that?" George asked Saint Peter. "Well, they were all together when a bad accident happened and as I was waiting to talk to them, I mentioned that you were here and they have been in that condition ever since." So, the moral of the story is not to be so quick to judge your neighbor.

Horizon 2012 has started and we are going on Wednesdays this year. In December, we had a 2-day retreat for the American Indians. I was in contact with Cainey and Tommy by telephone, thanks to the chaplain, Duane B. as to what all they needed. They would have to have pencils, notebooks, paper etc. also food. The families of our group provided all the brisket, ham, potato salad, baked beans, sweet potatoes, corn and lots of pastries and other desserts. I brought all the food in with the help of Jim and some of the other Kairos volunteers. Cainey and the new guys attending the retreat were meeting in the leather shop. Four men from previous Kairos weekends were in charge of food preparation and serving and were set up in a room right next to the leather shop. The names of the men were: Tommy, the young man who escorted me to the television room upstairs and told me that this is where they bring all their dates; Rusty, who is part Indian yet looks like a typical cowboy you would picture on a cattle drive, much like Clint Eastwood. He is tough and wiry in appearance, yet I found him to be quite a gentleman. He is eager to serve and is always moving about and ready to work. He has sandy blond hair and a large moustache that spreads from one side of his face to the other side. Denny, who is Choctaw has brown hair that is thinning a bit and brown eyes, broad facial features and a square jaw. His demeanor is pleasant and he is respectful of others. Cainey once made me a pair of moccasins, but when I tried them on, they didn't fit because my feet were too wide and I knew how Cinderella's ugly stepsisters must have felt as they tried to get their feet into the glass slipper. Denny asked me if I had any Choctaw blood in me and when I said yes he told me Choctaws have wide feet and that's the reason they didn't fit. He then told me to look at his feet that, as he put it, were as wide as they were long. It made me laugh and he laughed with me. Tony is Muscalero Apache and has a sprinkling of silver in his jet- black hair, his eyes are brown and he is of medium build and in his mid to late forties. He is quite nice looking on the outside and just as nice inside. He has an engaging personality, as well as being intelligent and interesting to talk with. Tony told me that staying busy with his work in the leather shop helps him forget he's locked up. I believe Tony will be a productive citizen when his time comes for parole.

During the retreat these men did everything and would hardly let me lift a hand. So I just got to relax and visit with them. Cainey had us come into the room for introductions, where he and the new guys were meeting, for drum call in the mornings and a presentation ceremony at the end of the weekend. At the presentation ceremony, each new guy received a gift, as well as my husband Jim and I. Jim received a beaded key ring and I received a dream catcher both handmade by some of the guys. They are gifts we treasure. There was a lot of down time during the weekend, so we had lots of conversations among those of us handling the food preparation. I had the opportunity to share my faith with them and give my beliefs on subjects such as my being against abortion and the death penalty that they brought up. It was a time for sharing and witnessing to them.

We are starting our first Wednesday Horizon program for the year and I am looking forward to getting to know the young men who went through the retreat. When we got to the Kairos unit, the program had already started and tonight a leader from each recognized religion, by the prison, was explaining the beliefs to the entire group of men. They gave their presentation, and then opened the floor for questions. The Christian religion was first, presented by a young man named, Trevor, who did an excellent job. Next, Cainey presented the traditional ways of the American Indian religion, and he did a great job, as well. The Muslims had their turn and then the pagans. The pagan presenter was not real sure of himself and his explanations were rather weak. A lot of what they believe is made up, with no basis or foundation. But if you submit a set of rules that you believe in and go by, the prison has to recognize it as a religion. At the very least it was an interesting night. Next week we should be back to meeting with our groups. My knee is almost 100% so I'll be able to climb the stairs to the T.V. room with my Indian group. Around the first part of January we went to Davis Correctional Facility at the usual time and I took a book titled, <u>Indian Spirit</u>, I received at Christmas from my son, Adam and his family. It has some amazing pictures of famous Indian chiefs from pre-reservation days, and their words of wisdom and beliefs. Here I will quote Thomas Wildcat Alford of the Shawnee Tribe, "Do not wrong or hate your neighbor, for it is not him that you wrong, you wrong yourself."

I am in awe of the wisdom and the spirit, in the teachings of the Indian ways I am learning. The men in our group showed a lot of interest as they avidly thumbed through the book. After the smoke off, we all shared from the meditation book, the day's meditation, what it meant to us and how we can apply the teachings to our daily life. I was especially impressed with what the younger guys, River and Shade had to say. They told how they handle situations much differently than before they came into the program. They said they're learning to be gentle and that it doesn't mean you are weak; it takes a strong person to be gentle. I get the sense that Shade is trying really hard to shake his past. He has a quality of leadership and is serious about staying on the "red road." He is making the most of his time spent in prison, much like Cainey. He is a handsome young man with dark brown hair and deep brown eyes that have a softness to them. God often lets me see these young men not just as inmates, but also as their mother's baby boys. Freddy, who is Cheyenne, with prominent bone structure, especially his cheekbones, but has finer features than the others. His coloring is light, but his hair is jet black. He has a habit of licking his lips, which could be due to a medication he's taking or some drug he used in the past, or maybe he just likes to lick his lips. Anyway, Freddy always greets me with a cup of coffee and the question, "How long does it take to drive here from Norman?" and my answer, of course, is always the same. "About an hour and 15 minutes," I tell him. I think this is all he can think to say in hopes of striking up a conversation with me. I wish I had something else to tell him, but the truth is, unless we stop in Tecumseh for a cappuccino at the local convenience store, or the time we hit a coyote by the lake there's not much to tell. I guess that's something when you are where he is and see and do the same thing day after day after day. He has good manners and is very respectful and I can tell he tries hard to please others. River has broader features and his hair is dark brown, almost black, and very curly. I would imagine he is aware of his good looks, yet he isn't cocky or self-occupied in any way. He has a kind way with the others and myself. But like Cainey has told me, they are all on their best behavior when I'm there, and I'm not so naïve as to think that being "little angels" is what got them where they are, but God can change us all if we are willing to let Him. I do appreciate the respect they show me.

Before I had to leave I was asked by Cainey if Jim and I could help him out by finding out where they could buy some bath towels for a sale they wanted to have. The prison issued bath towels are not very big and of poor quality. We said we would see what we could come up with and found a pretty good towel for 5 dollars, which they can sell and make a profit. The company will ship them to the prison and the inmates can unload them. So this is the kind of things you get to help out with being a sponsor. We are happy to do this and thank God for our health and the means with which to do it.

Another Wednesday night at DCF, we started as usual with the smoke off. Then we discussed chapter 5 in the meditation book, which was about being positive and how our attitudes can change the course of our day. Shade told how he had started to pray the minute his eyes open in the morning. He shared that he asks the Creator to give him a good day, to let him help someone, with a word or good deed. This, he added, is not how he would have awakened a couple of years ago. Freddy shared that when he first came to the yard here at Davis Correctional Facility, he was mean and had a hard way about him. But since he has been in the program, others have commented on how peaceful and happy he looks. River and Shade, along with Lane, are now high school graduates. They said that having children is what has given them the desire to do well and desire to be successful productive citizens. I believe they are well on their way.

It was exciting to see a new brother join the group, a young man named Kevin. Kevin is nice looking like the others. There is a quietness about him that I believe comes from being shy. It is a little hard for him to share in the group, but I can tell he has much to add if he can overcome his shyness. With encouragement from the others, he will find confidence. And with them as good examples he will follow his path on the red road. He came over from Dick Conner Facility in Hominy, Oklahoma. It has a reputation as a pretty rough place to do your time and needless to say, Kevin was glad to be at Davis with the support of his Indian brothers. If a person is ever going to change for the better, they have to understand who they are, and that they are worthy of being loved. That is what the Horizon program is about as well as teaching life skills. Being loved has to come first, which is what the Kairos weekend is all about and then change will happen. My positive outlook is not because I am a bleeding heart or Pollyanna. It is because God has given me compassion and hope, that with Him all things are possible. Then last but not least, I am a witness to this fact. I have seen change happen over and over again. What God does, with the help of the men on the Kairos team and Cainey, is put these men on a straight path. They show them the path that leads to God, the Creator of us all, with love and the example of their own lives, as well as knowledge of their faith. I will keep doing what I do to the best of my ability because I believe that is what God requires of me. I have found this to be the answer to a full and happy life. If I can help someone by something as simple as a smile or as involved as preparing meals for those in prison, if I can lift another person's burden by being present to them, truly listening and praying for them, than I have led a happy life. I hope I am pleasing God and when I fall short, I remember that his Grace is sufficient. God the Creator is good all the time.

The towels have arrived with only 170 being sold, which was far fewer than we expected. In light of this, we had them sent to us personally rather than to the prison. We brought them with us on this particular Wednesday night. As we arrived, the Chaplain helped us to get them processed and they were stored in a front office until logistics could be worked out on how they would be distributed. As expected, most everything is a huge process within the prison system. The Chaplain, Jim, and I then headed down to the Kairos unit to begin the night's program and to give Cainey and the others the good news that the towels had arrived. On the way, the Chaplain explained to us that many of the inmates aged 40 and over had been shipped to another facility. Because of the leadership and good work Cainey had done with the young men in our group, they had hopes that he would be coming back. They were told that it was not in the Warden's authority to keep Cainey from being shipped but that he could possibly be returned to Davis within a month or so. Hopefully this will be the case, but you never know.

Recently Lane, who has taken the leadership role of the Indian brothers group, told me he received word that Cainey will not be coming back. He said he has much work to do at Oklahoma State Reformatory. So in all likelihood we may not see Cainey again, at least not in this life. My prayer is to see in Heaven one day him and all those with whom my Kairos journey has allowed me to cross paths.

I recently received a letter from Cainey. He apologized for not getting to tell us goodbye, but said there is no word in his language for goodbye anyway, so he said he would just see us later. I do hope so. He says he is well and happy and believes the guys are in good hands with Lane and the elders to guide them. When I meet with my Indian brothers we always end our prayer with the word *A-Ho*, which for me is much like saying *Amen*. Since I have written this as a prayer I will say *A-Ho* and I'll see you later.